RIVERS *and* LAKES

Richard Beatty

www.raintreepublishers.co.uk
Visit our website to find out more information about Raintree books.

To order:
☎ Phone 0845 6044371
🖨 Fax +44 (0) 1865 312263
✉ Email myorders@raintreepublishers.co.uk

Customers from outside the UK please telephone +44 1865 312262

Raintree is an imprint of Capstone Global Library Limited, a company incorporated in England and Wales having its registered office at 7 Pilgrim Street, London, EC4V 6LB – Registered company number: 6695582

Text © Capstone Global Library Limited 2011
First published in hardback in 2011
The moral rights of the proprietor have been asserted.

For The Brown Reference Group
Editorial Director: Lindsey Lowe
Managing Editor: Tim Harris
Editor: Jolyon Goddard
Original consultant: Dr. Mark Hostetler, Department of Wildlife Ecology and Conservation, University of Florida
Designers: Reg Cox, Joan Curtis
Picture Researcher: Clare Newman
Production Director: Alastair Gourlay
Printed in the USA

ISBN: 978 1 406 21838 1

14 13 12 11 10
10 9 8 7 6 5 4 3 2 1

British Library Cataloguing in Publication Data
Beatty, Richard.
  Rivers and lakes. -- 2nd ed. -- (Biomes atlases) 1. Stream ecology--Juvenile literature. 2. Lake ecology--Juvenile literature. 3. Streams--Juvenile literature. 4. Lakes--Juvenile literature. I. Title II. Series

  577.6'3-dc22
A full catalogue record for this book is available from the British Library.

The acknowledgments on p. 64 form part of this copyright page. Every effort has been made to contact copyright holders of material reproduced in this book. Any omissions will be rectified in subsequent printings if notice is given to the publisher.

Disclaimer
All the Internet addresses (URLs) given in this book were valid at the time of going to press. However, due to the dynamic nature of the Internet, some addresses may have changed, or sites may have changed or ceased to exist since publication. While the author and publisher regret any inconvenience this may cause readers, no responsibility for any such changes can be accepted by either the author or the publisher.

About this Book

This book's introductory pages describe the biomes of the world and then the river and lake biomes. The five chapters look at aspects of rivers, lakes, streams and ponds: climate, plants, animals, people and the future. Between the chapters are detailed maps that focus on important rivers and lakes. The map pages are shown in the contents in italics, *like this*. Exclamation-mark icons on the map pages draw attention to regions where the biome or its wildlife is under threat. Throughout the book you'll also find boxed stories or fact files about rivers and lakes. The icons here show what the boxes are about. Words in **bold** throughout the book are explained in the glossary at the end of the book. After the glossary is a list of books and websites for further research and an index, allowing you to locate subjects anywhere in the book.

 Climate

 People

 Plants

 Future

 Animals

 Facts

 Extinction

 Under Threat

Contents

BIOMES OF THE WORLD

Biologists divide the living world into major zones named biomes. Each biome has its own distinctive climate, plants and animals.

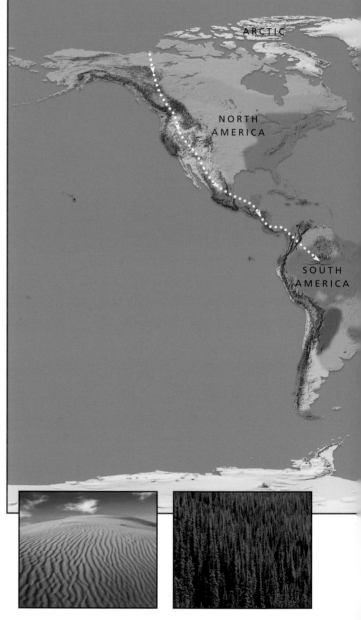

If you were to walk all the way from the north of Canada to the Amazon **rainforest**, you'd notice the wilderness changing dramatically along the way.

Northern Canada is a freezing and barren place without trees, where only tiny brownish-green plants can survive in the icy ground. But trudge south for long enough and you enter a magical world of conifer forests, where moose, caribou and wolves live. After several weeks, the conifers disappear, and you reach the grass-covered prairies of the central United States. The further south you go, the drier the land gets and the hotter the sunshine feels, until you find yourself hiking through a cactus-filled **desert**. But once you reach southern Mexico, the cacti start to disappear, and strange **tropical** trees begin to take their place. Here, the muggy air is filled with the calls of exotic birds and the drone of tropical insects. Finally, in Colombia you cross the Andes mountain range – whose chilly peaks remind you a little of your starting point – and descend into the dense, swampy jungles of the Amazon rainforest.

Desert is the driest biome. There are hot deserts and cold ones.

Taiga is made up of conifer trees that can survive freezing winters.

Scientists have a special name for the different regions – such as desert, tropical rainforest and prairie – that you'd pass through on such a journey. They call them **biomes**. Everywhere on Earth can be classified as being in one biome or another, and the same biome often appears in lots of

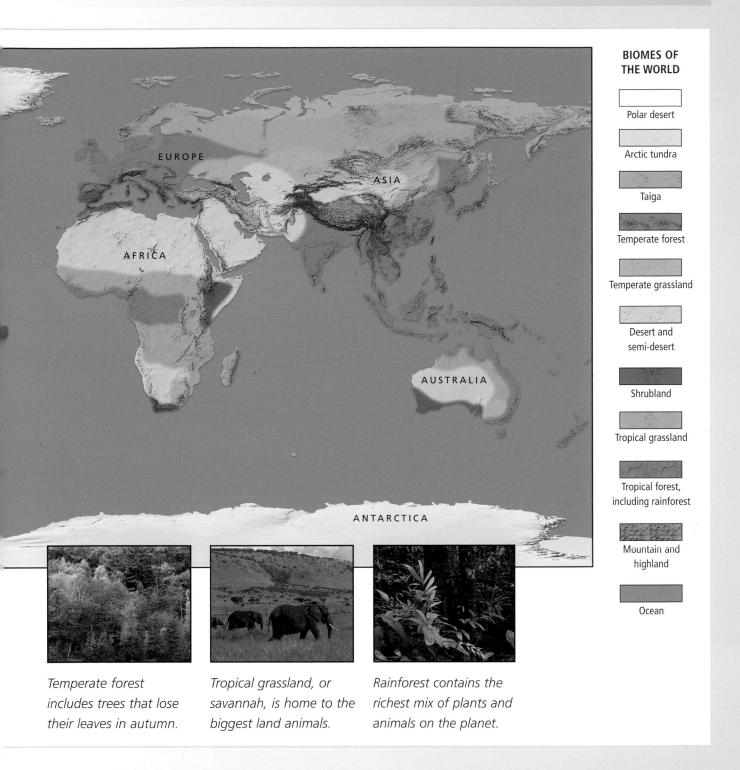

BIOMES OF THE WORLD

EUROPE

ASIA

AFRICA

AUSTRALIA

ANTARCTICA

☐	Polar desert
	Arctic tundra
	Taiga
	Temperate forest
	Temperate grassland
	Desert and semi-desert
	Shrubland
	Tropical grassland
	Tropical forest, including rainforest
	Mountain and highland
	Ocean

Temperate forest includes trees that lose their leaves in autumn.

Tropical grassland, or savannah, is home to the biggest land animals.

Rainforest contains the richest mix of plants and animals on the planet.

different places. For instance, there are areas of rainforest as far apart as Brazil, Africa and South-east Asia. Although the plants and animals that inhabit these forests are different, they live in similar ways. Likewise, the prairies of North America are part of the grassland biome, which also occurs in China, Australia and Argentina. Wherever there are grasslands, there are grazing animals that feed on the grass, as well as large carnivores that hunt and kill the grazers.

The map on this page shows how the world's major biomes fit together to make up the biosphere – the zone of life on Earth.

RIVERS AND LAKES OF THE WORLD

Rivers, lakes and other inland waters form one of the world's most varied biomes. From icy pools in the Arctic to enormous inland seas, and from mountain torrents to tropical rivers miles across, they provide a range of habitats for animals and plants.

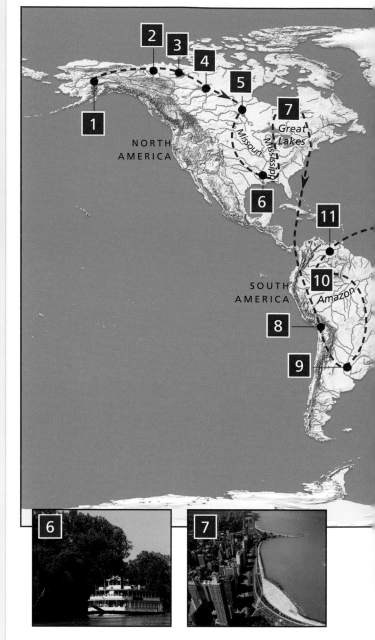

Barges and pleasure boats ply the great Mississippi waterway.

Water pollution has been a long-term problem in the Great Lakes.

The animals and plants of rivers and lakes do not live in the most stable of environments. Rivers and ponds may dry up altogether, while floods may alter rivers and valleys beyond recognition. Nonetheless, a great variety of creatures survive in this biome. Some 40 per cent of all **species** of fish live in **freshwater** – water with only a small amount of dissolved salt – although rivers and lakes cover a tiny area compared to oceans. Many great rivers start in mountains and highlands, such as the Chang (Yangtze) in China, which flows from the Tibetan Plateau, and the Ganges River of India, flowing from the Himalayas. Running down from the mountains, a river might reach any kind of landscape, from arctic tundra to baking desert. Those that flow through rainforest regions are fed by plentiful tropical rain and, like the Amazon and Congo rivers, become vast waterways miles across.

Wherever a depression in the land causes water to collect, a lake forms. Like rivers, most lakes are freshwater, and their animals and

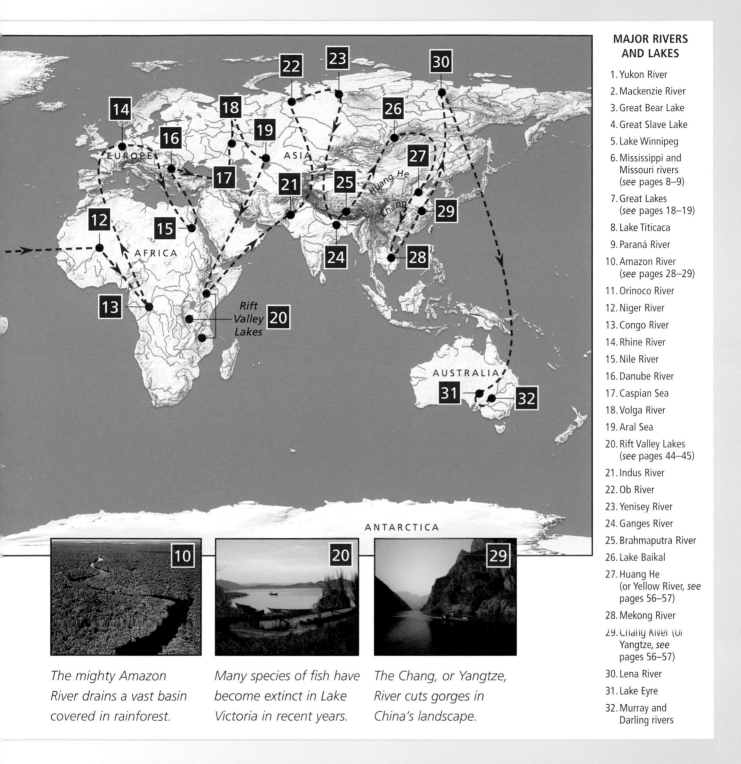

The mighty Amazon River drains a vast basin covered in rainforest.

Many species of fish have become extinct in Lake Victoria in recent years.

The Chang, or Yangtze, River cuts gorges in China's landscape.

plants differ from those of the great saltwater biome, the ocean. Many lakes are salty, though – sometimes much saltier than the sea and support only a small selection of creatures.

Rivers and lakes are unique in the way they affect nearby biomes. Rivers in flood vary the types of plants in valleys by creating marshes and swamps, while a desert stream may support the only trees for kilometres. Rivers can act as corridors for the movement of fish and waterbirds, but they can be barriers to land animals. However, it is **aquatic** wildlife that is truly isolated: it is a real challenge to travel to new rivers and lakes across barriers of land.

MISSISSIPPI

Forming the largest river system in North America, the Mississippi and its tributaries have played a central role in the history of the United States.

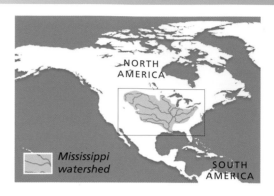

Mississippi
watershed

NORTH AMERICA

SOUTH AMERICA

Hurricane Katrina

Rivers usually run into the sea, but some weather conditions can cause the sea to flow upstream. When Hurricane Katrina hit New Orleans in 2005, it created a surge of seawater that travelled up the Mississippi River Gulf Outlet (an artificial waterway running through the city) and into other waterways. The surge caused more that 50 breaches in levees, or floodbanks, and 85 per cent of New Orleans was flooded. More than 1,000 people died, and the cost of repairing the damage ran into billions of pounds.

Engineers have built many structures across the river. Some generate electricity, others control flooding, but all of them obstruct the movement of wildlife.

Fact File

▲ The Mississippi system has the greatest diversity of freshwater mussels of any river system, with more than 60 species. At one time exploited for the pearl button industry, these mussels are now under threat. Pollution, competition from non-native species of mussels that have been introduced into the river, clogging by sediment and changes to river flow by dams all place the native mussels at risk.

▲ Much of North America was covered in ice during the last ice age, which ended about 10,000 years ago. The Mississippi Valley remained ice-free. When the ice age ended and the climate became warmer, fish and other aquatic animals from this region spread northwards and recolonised rivers and lakes that had previously been ice-bound.

An Alabama hog sucker (right) grazes algae from rocks in the clear, fast-running waters of the Tennessee river, which is a tributary of the Mississippi River. Young mussels live on the fish as parasites.

1. Missouri River
The Missouri and its tributary the Yellowstone carry sediment from the Rockies that causes the muddiness of the lower Mississippi. Farmland fertilisers entering the river cause bacterial overgrowth. Various stretches are no-go areas for swimmers.

2. Lake Itasca
This lake and the streams flowing into it are the source of the Mississippi River.

3. Chicago Sanitary and Ship Canal
This canal allows ships to pass between the Mississippi and the Great Lakes but has also allowed invasive pests such as the zebra mussel and Asian carp to spread.

In late 2009, Illinois state officials poisoned a stretch of the canal in order to kill Asian carp and stop their spread.

4. Cahokia
Once one of the largest cities of the Mississippian civilisation more than 800 years ago.

5. St. Louis
Despite being protected by high riverside banks (levees), St. Louis almost suffered disastrous flooding in the 1993 Mississippi floods. It was saved by a levee giving way on the far riverbank.

6. Bottomlands
The low-lying land where the Missouri and Mississippi meet was covered by distinctive forests and swamps. Most of these have been cleared, mainly for growing cotton and crops. The remaining forest is still under threat of deforestation.

7. Ohio River
This large tributary has suffered pollution from industrial activity in its basin near cities such as Pittsburgh and Cincinnati.

8. Appalachian, Ozark, and Ouachita Highlands
Stretches of river unmodified by dams in these highlands are rich in wildlife. Here live many species of snails, mussels and crayfish and, in the larger rivers, ancient types of fish such as sturgeons and paddlefish.

9. Mississippi Delta
The Mississippi has changed its outlet to the sea several times in the last few thousand years.

10. Dead Zone
Pollution in the Mississippi causes the oxygen content of its waters to be low. Where the oxygen-poor Mississippi water enters the ocean, it causes a dead zone, where marine life cannot flourish. Scientists are hopeful that the dead zone can be revived.

STILL AND FLOWING WATERS

From whitewater rapids to placid lakes, rivers and lakes create a wealth of habitats for wildlife. They also play a vital role in Earth's water cycle and help shape the landscape.

Without the heat from the Sun driving the world's weather systems, Earth's land surface would be dry and lifeless. The water that **evaporates** (turns to **vapour**) from the ocean later falls as rain or snow and makes life on land possible. Some of the water soaks deep into the ground. Another fraction of the water is taken up by plants or evaporates again. But much of it finds its way into rivers, the land's natural drains. It flows downhill until it reaches the lowest level – usually the sea, but sometimes an inland lake. Worldwide, this sequence of events is known as the water cycle.

Rivers vary greatly. Some are fed by a very small area – the side of a snowcapped mountain, for example – while others collect water from a vast area of land. The area that a river drains is called its **watershed**. In a large watershed, there may be dozens of small rivers and streams, or **tributaries**, flowing into the main river. Together, these rivers and streams make up a river system.

The Amazon river system has the biggest watershed of all, covering about one-third of South America. The watershed of the Mississippi river system is nearly as big, but this system carries only about one-tenth as much water as the Amazon because far less rain falls there than in South America.

Some rivers, such as the Rhine River in Europe, flow fairly evenly throughout the year. Others have annual floods, driven either by the spring thaw in cooler **climates** or by a rainy season. Some rivers even freeze over during winter. Rivers also vary a lot in the amount of **sediment** (sand and mud particles) they carry. The Mississippi and the Amazon are both very muddy rivers, for example. Many of their fish find their way using smell and touch rather than sight.

The Long Term

Rivers slowly wear away the ground and, over millions of years, reshape the landscape. High mountains and highlands, pushed up by forces deep inside Earth, are ground down by

Fact File

▲ Lakes are not lakes forever: even large lakes fill slowly with sediment and disappear. By far the oldest is Lake Baikal in Siberia, at 25 million years old. Most lakes are less than 12,000 years old. Searles Lake in the Mojave Desert, California, is now dried up. It was about 200 metres (660 feet) deep thousands of years ago.

▲ Waterfalls are natural barriers to fish and other animals that cannot reach the river or lake habitat above a cascade. Aquatic wildlife must now face new obstructions, such as dams and other artificial structures.

The ancient, hard rock of the Grand Teton range in Wyoming (background) is not easily worn away by streams and rivers. As a result, the water of the Snake River (foreground) is often clear and free of fine sediment.

Fact File

▲ Rivers are natural water courses, usually containing freshwater, that flow toward an ocean, sea, or lake or into another river.

▲ Lakes are large bodies of water situated inland. Most are freshwater; some are salty.

▲ Streams are small rivers.

▲ Ponds are small bodies of water.

glaciers, split by frost or worn down by rivers and wind. Streams and rivers carry away the crumbling material, carving out valleys as they do so. New mountains form as old ones wear away, so the cycle continues.

The result of these ongoing processes is a patchwork of watersheds, each drained by a different river system and separated by higher ground. In the United States, the Rocky Mountains form a barrier that separates rivers draining westward towards the Pacific Ocean from those flowing east into the Mississippi. For aquatic (water-dwelling) animals, crossing from one watershed to another may be impossible. As a result, many river systems contain unique species that **evolved** within them and that live nowhere else.

A river system may have a complex history. Millions of years ago, for example, sea levels rose and dammed back the water of the Amazon river system, so much of the watershed turned into a kind of swampy lake. Later, during the ice age (a period when Earth's climate became much colder), sea levels were much lower than today, and the Amazon's river valleys became deep ravines.

River water ranges from clear to muddy and from energetic to sluggish. Chinook salmon (above) must swim against the raging torrents of mountain rivers, dodging waiting brown bears. Catfish (below) have their own problems – to find their way through murky water they need long, sensitive barbels (fleshy whiskers).

Today, these canyons are invisible, drowned by sediment or filled with water more than 90 metres (300 feet) deep.

Sometimes a river keeps cutting down into its valley while the land around is rising; the Grand Canyon in Arizona is the most spectacular result of this process. In other regions, such as the Great Lakes, the whole area was buried under solid ice during the ice age. The animals now living in the region arrived during the last 15,000 years, after the ice finally melted.

Compared to rivers, which flowed through watersheds long before the ice age, most lakes are relatively young features of Earth's surface. They tend to fill in with sediment

world's oldest and deepest lakes have a different origin. In areas such as East Africa, movements in Earth's crust created vast splits in the land that filled with water and formed deep lakes; some are now several million years old. A lake can also form in a valley that has been blocked by a landslide, in the crater of a volcano, or occasionally in an old meteor crater.

Rushing Waters

Rivers and streams provide many different kinds of habitats for animals and plants. The way the water flows has a huge influence on the kinds of creatures that can survive in it. Most rivers start as swift-flowing streams among hills or mountains. The churning rapids capture plenty of oxygen from the air, helping fish and other aquatic animals breathe underwater. Getting a meal, though, can be a challenge. Few plants can avoid being swept away by the powerful current – and in any case, there is usually no mud in which to take root.

brought by rivers. Most of the world's lakes were created by glaciers during the ice age. Glaciers are slow-flowing rivers of ice that scour great hollows out of the land as they move. North America's Great Lakes formed this way. However, some of the

Feeling the Heat

You might not think that anything could survive in the hot, salty springs of volcanic areas such as Yellowstone Park (left), but a few organisms can. Bacteria form the base of food chains. Many of these bacteria are cyanobacteria, which like plants use sunlight to make their own food. Insects such as water beetles and midge larvae also thrive in the springs. There are even tiny worms that can stand temperatures of 60°C (140°F) – more than halfway to the boiling point of water.

Without plants, there can be no plant-eating animals for the fish to eat.

The biggest source of food in a stream is not plants but waste material from outside the stream. Especially where a stream runs through a forest, dead leaves and rotting wood fall into the water and form the starting point for a **community** of living things, beginning with fungi and **bacteria** and other micro-organisms that break down

A stream that flows through a tropical forest picks up a steady supply of dead plant parts, dead animals and faeces from above. All the animals in the stream rely on this material, directly or indirectly, for food.

the dead material. These organisms, which form the slime around rocks and leaves in streams, are the main food source for aquatic larvae (young stages) of insects. Mayfly larvae, for instance, scrape the slime off rocks and

A World of Darkness

A river can disappear underground wherever a hole or crack lets the water through. It may continue flowing underground, and over thousands of years, it can carve a system of caves through the rock. Such caves might seem cut off from the life-giving light and warmth of the Sun, but life continues in the darkness. Cave animals live on morsels of food carried by the river water from the sunlit biomes above. The top predators in caves are often blind cave fish (left).

eat it but in turn become a meal for predators such as water beetles, water bugs and fish.

Flowing Smoothly

As a stream or river reaches lower ground, its slope gets gentler and the water flow becomes smoother. It may still flow fast, but near the riverbed there is calmer water that allows sand and mud to settle. Animals such as worms and mussels bury themselves in the bed and filter mud and water for small food particles. Waterweeds may take root, trailing their long stems in the water, while tall plants such as reeds often grow around the water's edge. Other rivers are too deep or muddy for underwater plants to grow.

Some rivers fall from great heights, forming thundering waterfalls. A large waterfall can create its own mini-environment, where the air is constantly filled with mist and spray. It can also provide hiding places: South America's massive Iguaçú Falls shelter a type of swift. This bird can dive straight through the curtain of water with its wings folded before finding a safe perch on the rock behind.

A river nearing the sea usually slows and deposits sediment. Banks of sediment can serve as turtle nesting sites or as places for crocodiles to beach themselves.

Many rivers, such as the Mississippi, flood in their lower course, forming a patchwork of marshes, shallow lakes and other habitats.

Like other waterfalls, Iguaçú Falls in southern Brazil form a barrier that many river animals cannot cross.

The Amazon River floods a huge area of forest every year; the trees have evolved to survive being flooded for months at a time. Many fish swim into the forest at this time to feed. Some trees drop their fruit during the flood and depend on fish to eat and distribute the seeds.

Eventually, the river reaches the sea. The mixing of salt water and freshwater, the rise and fall of the tides, and the muddy particles that settle on the river bottom create a variety of special habitats. Broad mudflats may glisten at low tide, hiding countless small creatures that sift through the mud for detritus (pieces

Lakes in Sweden usually freeze over in winter. Birds cannot reach food such as fish and water plants. Most animals beneath the ice decrease activity until spring.

of dead material). If the river brings enough mud and there is no powerful sea current to take it away, it may build its own flatland (a **delta**) far out at sea. Lagoons, brackish (semi-salty) marshes, and sometimes mangrove swamps also contribute to the natural variety at the river's end.

How Lakes Work

Compared with rivers and streams, lakes (especially large ones) depend more on food produced in the water itself than on dead material falling in from the shore. As in the sea, the **food chains** depend mainly on microscopic floating **algae** and cyanobacteria, or **phytoplankton**. Phytoplankton grow only in the upper layer of the lake, where there is enough light. They need chemicals called **nutrients**, which are dissolved in the water. The nutrients determine how many phytoplankton can survive. Scotland's Loch Ness, for example, is very low in nutrients, so there are few phytoplankton. It would be very difficult for Loch Ness's legendary monster to find enough to eat in such infertile water.

 Mud Records of the Past

Scientists can find out a lot by studying sediments at the bottom of lakes. These may date back thousands of years and are sometimes laid down yearly in layers called varves, like the rings built up yearly by growing trees. The sediments preserve the remains of plankton from the water and pollen from nearby forests that may no longer exist. The records allow scientists to reconstruct the history of the area. They can also record onetime events, such as ash from an ancient volcano or recent radioactive pollution.

The way the waters of a lake mix – or don't mix – greatly affects the lake's life. The Sun warms the surface water. Because warm water is less dense than cold water, it floats on top as a separate layer. This top layer has plenty of oxygen because the waves mix with the air. This is good for the animals that live there but as they grow, they use up nutrients, and when they die, they sink to the layer below. The upper layer can therefore be very low in nutrients. The layer below is just the opposite: it has less opportunity to receive oxygen and can't support very much life, but it has plenty of nutrients.

In cooler countries, the warm surface layer forms in summer but disappears in fall, and winter winds can mix the lake waters completely. If ice forms, the waters mix a second time in spring, when the ice melts. Thanks to the frequent mixing, oxygen is available deep down, allowing burrowing animals such as worms to survive in the mud.

In tropical lakes, the layers may be almost permanent. The deep water is not only cooler but has far less oxygen – sometimes so little that only micro-organisms can survive. When dead matter sinks to the lake floor, the micro-organisms break it down and release poisons such as hydrogen sulfide. On the rare occasions when such tropical lake water mixes, millions of fish may die as the rising stagnant water suffocates and poisons them.

Near the edge of a lake, the water may be sufficiently shallow and well-lit for reeds and other plants to take root in the muddy bottom. The shallows are often ideal habitats for insects, snails and other creatures, and the plants provide hiding places for fish. In other parts of the lakeshore, though, waves and wind may prevent plants from growing, making these rocky shores look barren.

Salt Lakes

Although most lakes contain freshwater, some contain water as salty as the sea – or even saltier. The world's largest salt lake, the Caspian Sea, was once joined to the ocean. Today, it still contains mainly marine organisms.

Most salt lakes lie far from the sea, however, and are salty because, like the Caspian Sea, they have no outlet. Rivers that drain into lakes always bring some dissolved salts with them, so a lake only stays fresh if it also has an outlet, allowing the salts to wash away. Otherwise the salt has nowhere to go and gradually builds up. Sometimes the main salt is common salt (sodium chloride), but other lakes contain mainly soda (sodium carbonate), which makes the lake alkaline. (An alkali is the opposite of an acid.) Most fish cannot survive in very salty or alkaline water, but some phytoplankton, shrimps and other animals thrive in such habitats. With little competition, they multiply in lakes such as Utah's Great Salt Lake. In East Africa's soda lakes, cyanobacteria and shrimps feed millions of flamingos (below).

GREAT LAKES

The Great Lakes of North America hold nearly one-fifth of Earth's surface freshwater. The hollows now occupied by the lakes were carved out during several ice ages.

Isle Royale, the land stretching across the top of the picture, lies in Lake Superior and is home to timber wolves and moose. It became a world biosphere reserve in 1980.

1. Boundary Waters
Thousands of smaller lakes on the Minnesota–Ontario border draw canoeists in search of wilderness adventures. Few anglers reach the more remote lakes, where smallmouth bass, northern pike, walleye and lake trout are all abundant.

2. Isle Royale National Park
The islands of this park are surrounded by shipwrecks now explored by divers.

3. Keweenaw National Historical Park
Copper has been extracted here by Native Americans since 7,000 years ago. The park also preserves relics of what was the world's most important source of copper in the 19th century.

4. Lake Superior
The world's largest freshwater lake by area, Lake Superior is the size of South Carolina. The lake stores more water than all the other Great Lakes put together. It is called 'Superior' because it is the highest Great Lake above sea level. At up to 407 metres (1,333 feet) deep, it is also the deepest. In the last 30 years, the lake's average summer temperature has risen by 2.5°C (4.5°F) because of global warming.

5. Lake Michigan
With a coastline ranging from marshes and prairies to sand dunes, Lake Michigan's ecology is varied. Chicago and other cities lie on its shores. It is nearly as large as West Virginia. Invasive zebra mussels and lampreys out-compete and harm native animals.

6. Sleeping Bear Dunes National Lakeshore
The lakeside dunes tower up to 140 metres (460 feet) above Lake Michigan's waters.

7. Fathom Five National Marine Park
This underwater park preserves evidence of the Great Lakes' history, including a huge former waterfall that once allowed Lake Huron's waters to reach the sea via the Ottawa River.

 Fact File

▲ The Great Lakes absorb and store so much heat from the surrounding air that they cause cooler summers than in prairie lands further west. They slowly release this heat in fall, causing milder winters than in the prairies.

▲ Eutrophication is the build-up of nutrients, often from agricultural fertilisers washed into lakes, that causes bacterial overgrowth, which stifles other freshwater life. It is a problem in the Great Lakes.

▲ The easy transportation of grain, coal, copper and other commodities via the Great Lakes was a major factor in the industrial and agricultural development of the United States.

NORTH AMERICA

0   200 miles
0   200 kilometres

N

Right: the American Falls at Niagara do not have the spectacular horseshoe shape of Niagara's Canadian Falls, but at 51 metres (167 feet), they are a little taller.

12

Hudson Bay   QUEBEC

Lake Nipigon

Ouimet Canyon

C A N A D A

ONTARIO

Thunder Bay **!** **4**

Pukaskwa National Park

Lake Superior

Lake Superior National Park

Quetico Provincial Park
Voyageurs National Park
Boundary Waters

1

2

Isle Royale National Park (U.S.)

3

Whitefish Bay

MICHIGAN

North Channel
Manitoulin Is.

Killarney National Park

Georgian Bay Island National Park

Ottawa River

Apostle Islands National Lakeshore

Keweenaw National Historical Park

Green Bay

Fathom Five National Marine Park

Bruce Peninsula National Park

Georgian Bay

Haliburton Highlands

Ottawa

Minneapolis

!

5

6

Sleeping Bear Dunes

7

8

Niagara Escarpment

St. Lawrence Islands National Park

St. Lawrence River

WISCONSIN

MINNESOTA

Mississippi River

Milwaukee

Lake Michigan

Lake Huron

Toronto

13 **!**

Lake Ontario

Lake St. Clair

ONTARIO

Buffalo **12**

Niagara Falls

IOWA

ILLINOIS
Chicago

Indiana Dunes

Detroit

9

MICHIGAN

Point Pelee National Park

!

10 **Lake Erie**

Mayfly plague area

11

NEW YORK

PENNSYLVANIA

U N I T E D   S T A T E S

OHIO
Cleveland

8. Lake Huron
This lake has around 90,000 islands and is almost cut in two by a ridge of hard rock called the Niagara Escarpment, which also forms Niagara Falls.

9. Point Pelee National Park
Canada's southernmost point is a major center for migrating birds, as well as containing broad-leaved forest that was once widespread in the region.

10. Lake Erie
The shallowest of the Great Lakes, Lake Erie is bordered by cities such as Detroit and Cleveland. Pollution increased after 1950 and led to one of the lake's inlets catching fire due to all the oily pollutants it carried. A campaign to clean up the lake was launched and some native fish have now returned to the lake.

11. Mayfly Plague
Lake Erie has been cleaned so successfully that the larvae (young forms) of mayflies are again abundant in the lake. In summer, the adults emerge from the lake and swarm in huge numbers. They quickly mate, lay eggs and die, their bodies piling up in heaps.

12. Niagara Falls
These famous falls are slowly moving upstream as the water erodes the underlying rocks. The nearby Welland Canal allows ships to bypass the falls and reach Lake Erie.

13. Lake Ontario
Lying below Niagara Falls, Lake Ontario has always been more accessible to fish and other animals that reach it from the sea via the St. Lawrence River. Eutrophication has been a problem in Lake Ontario.

Changing Ecology

At the end of the last ice age, fish colonised the newly ice-free Great Lakes, while trees took over most of the nearby land. When Europeans began to settle in the 1700s, they cut down many of the forests, choking tributary streams with sawdust so fish such as trout and sturgeon could no longer lay eggs there. The lakes provided commercial fishers with large catches of trout and plankton-eating fish such as whitefish and lake herring, but overfishing meant that by the middle of the 20th century these catches were declining. The Welland Canal also allowed in alien species such as the sea lamprey (below), an invader that eats the native fish alive.

WATER PLANTS

From microscopic plankton to towering palm trees, many plants or plant-like organisms make their home in rivers and lakes. Water is seldom in short supply, but getting enough light, air and nutrients can be a challenge.

Plants growing in water face a different world from their land-living relatives. One crucial challenge they face is getting oxygen. Water plants need to breathe air, just as we do, but they often grow in mud that contains none of this vital element at all. Many of them make up for this with air-filled stems and leafstalks. These transport oxygen down to their roots – and often help keep the plants from sinking in the water as well.

Plants need light, but light can be in short supply underwater. In streams, there's also the constant danger of being washed away by the current. On the other hand, the biggest challenge to land plants – getting enough water – is much less of a problem for aquatic plants. In fact, most water plants can take in water through their leaves and stems, rather than relying only on their roots. If a pond does dry out, though, some species become temporary land plants, growing toughened leaves that resist wilting in air.

Small and Simple

Among the most important life-forms in freshwater are algae – a name given to a wide range of organisms, from microscopic single cells to giant seaweeds – and cyanobacteria (which used to be called blue-green algae). These are not plants. However, like plants, they use the Sun's energy to synthesise their own food, a chemical process called photosynthesis.

Most freshwater algae are the microscopic, single-celled variety. In lakes particularly, these play a crucial role in the **plankton** – a community of tiny, free-floating organisms that forms the basis of food chains in both the sea and freshwater. Planktonic algae are also called phytoplankton (plant-like plankton) to distinguish them from zooplankton (animal-like plankton). Other types of algae grow attached to rocks or the surface of larger plants, where they are sometimes visible as a fuzzy green layer.

Insects such as this honeybee find floating water plants handy as a secure platform on which to drink.

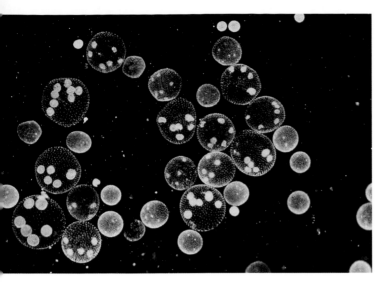

Microscopically tiny algae called volvox form ball-shaped colonies less than 1 millimetre (0.04 inches) across. They float in the water like little green jewels.

Freshwater phytoplankon are very diverse. The smallest are cyanobacteria, which sometimes multiply until they form a thick green scum on the water. Cyanobacteria were once called blue-green algae, but they are neither true plants nor true algae. Instead, they are considered to be types of bacteria (though very different from the bacteria that cause human diseases). Other microscopic algae, called diatoms, are noted for making beautiful, glass-like shells out of silica, the same substance that sand is made of.

In many lakes, there is a spring bloom of phytoplankton growth, fuelled by increasing light and warmth. When phytoplankton use up the lake's nutrients, the bloom finishes and the remains of dead phytoplankton fall to the lake bed.

Larger Plants

Most large freshwater plants are flowering plants, which have dominated plant life since they first evolved more than 100 million years ago. In a few freshwater habitats, such as mountain streams, moss, ferns and other non-flowering species can also be common.

Freshwater flowering plants evolved from various land-living families. They are easier to describe in terms of the way they grow rather than in terms of the families of plants they belong to. For example, plants such as reeds, which grow through shallow water and into the air, are known as **emergents**. In deeper water, these are usually replaced by plants such as water lilies, which have floating leaves but roots that are anchored in the bed. Other plants float freely on the surface with dangling roots, and some live entirely underwater. Finally, some plants are adapted to life in fast streams, either clinging tightly to rocks or growing long, flexible stems that wave in the current.

Reeds, cattails, and other emergents can form dense stands along the edge of a river or lake. They spread quickly, sending horizontal stems (**rhizomes**) through the mud. At intervals, the stems produce new shoots – the parts you see above water. On the edge of a pond, the dead remains of emergent plants can build up to form a waterlogged soil called peat. Peat is very fibrous and micro-organisms can't break it down due to the lack of oxygen. Peat builds along the pond edges, and the pond may gradually fill up. Trees and shrubs may take over, forming a swamp or even dry land.

 New to Science

Arsenic is a chemical that is poisonous to humans. It is found naturally in the ground and also in many ponds and rivers. In 2009, a Californian engineer discovered that cattails remove up to 90 per cent of the arsenic in freshwater. They absorb the chemical as though it were a nutrient and are not damaged by it. The discovery of this natural water-filtration system may help millions of people in developing nations, whose water supplies are contaminated with arsenic.

Common reeds are emergent water plants, rooting themselves in water shallow enough for their stems to reach high above the water and breathe in the air.

Water lilies, probably the best known water plants, also grow using rhizomes. The rhizomes store food and are eaten by people in some parts of the world. The biggest species – the giant Victoria lily of the Amazon – has round, tray-shaped leaves up to 2 metres (6.5 feet) wide.

Water lilies breathe through tiny airholes on the upper surface of their leaves; the leaves produce wax, which prevents the leaves from filling with water. Other plants that usually have floating leaves include water crowfoots (relatives of the buttercups), duckweeds and pondweeds, which are often important food for ducks.

Many mosses cling to stones around the damp edges of mountain streams and waterfalls, although a few live their whole lives underwater. Mosses are important to small animals because they provide shelter from the current.

Around tropical waterfalls and rapids you can also find some very weird flowering plants that glue themselves flat to rocks to avoid being swept away. Known as podostemons, they look like green chewing gum – except in the dry season, when the 'chewing gum' starts sprouting flowers.

Right: mosses flourish on the water-splashed rocks beside many mountain streams and provide shelter for a host of tiny aquatic creatures.

Sacred Flower

The sacred lotus of Asia is a water plant with large emergent leaves and flowers like those of a water lily. It is regarded as sacred in the Buddhist religion and has appeared in countless religious drawings and carvings. There is also a lotus flower native to North America. Some botanists regard this as a sub-species of the sacred lotus, while others consider it a separate species.

The duckweed family includes Earth's smallest flowering plants. Valdivia duckweed (above) is one of the tiniest. The rice grain in the centre shows just how small it is.

Floaters and Sinkers

Plants that float freely in the water risk being swept away, so they thrive best in still waters. They also need nutrient-rich water, because their roots are not in contact with soil or mud. Under the right conditions, however, they can entirely cover the surface of ponds and ditches, smothering other plants and preventing oxygen from reaching the water below. Floating plants include many species that are now invasive pests, such as water hyacinth, water lettuce and several floating ferns. They also include the miniature duckweeds. The whole body of a duckweed is a few tiny, floating oval leaves bearing a few small roots. *Wolffia* duckweed has leaves less than 1 millimetre (0.04 inches) long.

The most specialised water plants are those that live completely submerged. They often grow in shady places and must absorb all their oxygen and other gases from the water. Often these submerged plants have finely divided leaves that help them absorb gases and nutrients. Among the most widespread are the milfoils (a name coming from the French for a thousand leaves'), including the native American northern milfoil and its invasive Eurasian cousin, the spiked milfoil.

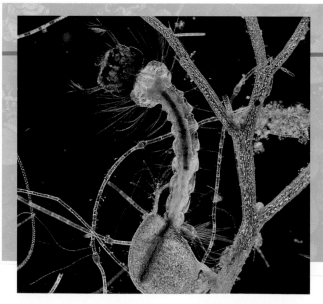

 ## Floating Ambush

Bladderwort is the only carnivorous (animal-eating) plant that lives underwater. Floating just below the surface in ponds, it grows small swellings called bladders. If an animal, such as a mosquito larva (left) or a water flea, bumps into a bladder, it is sucked in, trapped and later digested, providing the plant with useful nutrients such as nitrogen. Although there are other carnivorous plants, they all grow in bogs or fens rather than in open water. They all trap insects to get nutrients not present in the soil.

Water crowfoots have some of the prettiest of all water flowers. They are like buttercups with floating leaves and flowers, and they bloom in clean freshwater.

The Next Generation

Like plants on land, aquatic flowering plants can reproduce either sexually – via flowers and seeds – or asexually. **Asexual reproduction** can be accomplished by creeping stems or roots, or it can simply rely on small fragments of the plant breaking off and taking root elsewhere. Such asexual methods are particularly common in water plants, probably because it's easy for plant fragments to float away to new habitats without drying out on the way.

Besides helping plants spread, asexual reproduction can help them survive being frozen and broken apart in winter. Many water plants produce specialised winter buds called turions, which can survive on the bottom of a pond below the surface ice while the rest of the plant dies. In the case of a common floating plant called water soldier, the whole plant sinks to the bottom before sprouting smaller plants at the end of short stems. In spring, they return to the surface, where they give rise to a new generation.

Most water plants, even submerged ones, produce their flowers above water. They rely on wind or insects to transfer the **pollen** (which contains the male sex cells) from one flower to another, a process called **pollination**. When the female part of a flower is pollinated, a seed develops within it. Plants such as reeds and cattails are wind-pollinated; their small flowers produce dusty pollen that can blow for miles in the wind. Water lilies and other species with showy flowers rely on insects to pick up sticky pollen. They attract the insects with scent, colourful petals, and a sugary secretion called nectar. Some water lilies even generate heat as an attraction.

A few water plants, including one called hornwort or coontail, have gone one step further: they flower underwater. Such plants produce thread-like pollen that can wrap around the female parts of flowers. Another plant – water celery – produces male flowers that detach and float to the surface like tiny boats. These drift until they reach a female flower (which remains anchored), allowing pollination to take place.

After pollination, the flowers of aquatic plants may withdraw underwater to protect the growing seeds. The stalks of water lily

Water milfoils can live completely submerged. The pictured species is native to South America, but it has escaped from aquariums in the United States.

AMAZON

The sheer scale of the Amazon River is awe inspiring. One-fifth of all the world's river water passes between its banks.

Even small tributaries in the Amazon river system are major rivers (below). They provide a system of watery highways, useful for travel in a region with few roads.

Fact File

▲ The Nile may be longer than the Amazon, but the Amazon is definitely Earth's greatest river – it drains the largest river basin in the world.

▲ In the 21st century, drought – probably caused by deforestation and global warming – has been a growing problem in the Amazon region.

▲ The Amazon provides some unusual habitats: Plants float on the river, forming islands that may be more than 0.8 kilometres (0.5 miles) long. They sink and decay during the dry season.

Left: at up to 1.8 metres (6 feet) long, the Amazon's giant otter is a powerful killer that can hunt in packs to drive fish towards riverbanks.

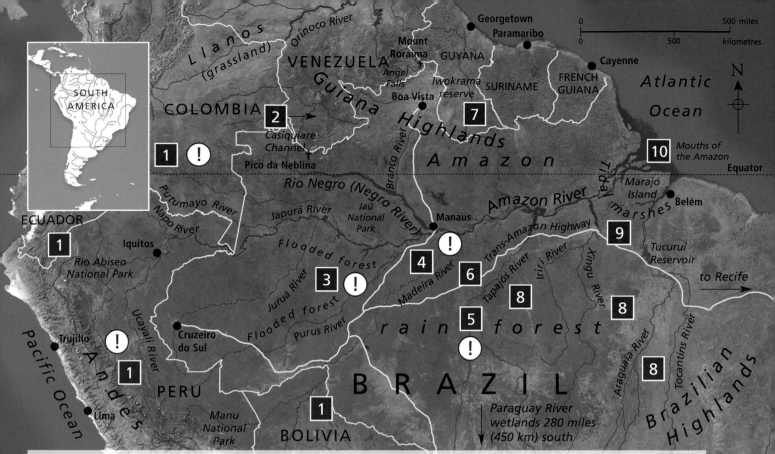

Map labels:

Llanos (grassland)
Orinoco River
VENEZUELA
Mount Roraima
Georgetown
Paramaribo
GUYANA
Cayenne
Angel Falls
Iwokrama reserve
SURINAME
FRENCH GUIANA
Atlantic Ocean
COLOMBIA
Guiana Highlands
Boa Vista
2
Casiquiare Channel
7
1 !
Pico da Neblina
Amazon
10 Mouths of the Amazon
Equator
ECUADOR
Putumayo River
Napo River
Rio Negro (Negro River)
Branco River
Manaus
Amazon River
Tidal marshes
Marajó Island
Belém
1
Iquitos
Japurá River
Jaú National Park
Rio Abiseo National Park
Flooded forest
4 !
Madeira River
6
Trans-Amazon Highway
Tapajós River
Iriri River
Xingu River
9
Tucurui Reservoir
Juruá River
3 !
Flooded forest
Purus River
5 !
r a i n   f o r e s t
8
8
to Recife
Ucayali River
Cruzeiro do Sul
B R A Z I L
Trujillo !
Andes
1
PERU
Manu National Park
BOLIVIA
1
Araguaia River
Tocantins River
8
Brazilian Highlands
Lima
Paraguay River wetlands 280 miles (450 km) south
Pacific Ocean
Brasília
SOUTH AMERICA
0   500 miles
0   500 kilometres
N

1. Amazon Headwaters
Many Amazon tributaries begin up in the Andes of Bolivia, Peru, Ecuador and Colombia. Even in minor tributaries there are many fish species. Glaciers that feed the Amazon River are retreating because of global warming.

2. Casiquiare Channel
A natural river connection between the Rio Negro and the Orinoco River to the north. Such a connection between two watersheds is very unusual. It is up to 533 metres (1,750 feet) wide. In flood, it flows at 8 km/h (5 mph) toward the Rio Negro.

3. Flooded Forest
The Amazon and many of its tributaries flood every year. In the flooded areas, trees grow that can tolerate being in up to 12 metres (40 feet) of water for several months of the year. Deforestation is a threat to this unique habitat.

4. Madeira River
The valley of this tributary is a flyway for waterbirds migrating between the Amazon and the Paraguay River wetlands. Pollution coming from gold mining is a growing problem in the Madeira River.

5. Amazon Rainforest
The Amazon drains the greatest rainforest in the world. Despite rapid deforestation, much of this forest is still intact.

6. Trans-Amazon Highway
This road has opened much of the previously remote Amazon region, with effects that include leakages of poisonous mercury into rivers from gold mining.

7. Iwokrama Reserve
Part of the effort to protect Earth's largest freshwater fish – the endangered 2-metre (7-foot) arapaima.

8. Clear-water Rivers
A diverse range of fish migrate in vast numbers up and down clear rivers such as the Xingu, Araguaia and Tapajós.

9. Tidal Marshes
Ocean tides push back the Amazon's waters daily. They create tidal forests and marshes that are flooded with river water twice a day up to 400 kilometres (260 miles) inland.

10. Mouths of the Amazon
The strength of the Amazon's current carries its waters 320 kilometres (200 miles) out to sea.

Threatened Fish

The arapaima is a giant Amazon River fish that grows to 2 metres (7 feet) long and can weigh up to 200 kilograms (440 pounds). A study published in 2010 suggests that there are several species of the fish rather than just one, as previously believed. The fish are threatened with extinction mainly because they are overfished – their flesh is very tasty. Unusually for fish, arapaima breathe at the water's surface, which makes them even more vulnerable to harpoon and gill-net fishers.

WATER ANIMALS

Freshwater habitats contain an amazing variety of animals. Most are invaders – animals whose ancestors entered freshwater from either the ocean or from land.

In the course of evolution, animals tend to move into new regions and adapt over many generations to their new environment. For sea-living animals, making the move to freshwater has its challenges. Freshwater habitats are more changeable than the sea – they may freeze, turn into raging torrents, lose all their oxygen or even dry up. There are also problems caused by the lack of salt. While seawater has about the same salt concentration as the fluid in animals' bodies, freshwater is much less salty. The salty fluid in an animal's body tends to absorb freshwater, making the body fluid too watery. Small animals are always in danger of water flooding into their tissues, making them swell up and even burst.

As a result of these challenges, not all sea animals have made the leap to living in lakes and rivers. While there are freshwater crabs in many parts of the world, you don't find freshwater starfish or freshwater octopuses.

Water animals whose ancestors lived on land include insects and most freshwater snails, in addition to mammals such as otters. To live in freshwater, all such animals need to return to the water surface to breathe air, unless during millions of years of evolution in freshwater, they have developed gills. Gills are feathery organs divided into a myriad of tiny branches. They have an enormous surface area, and they allow dissolved gases – oxygen and **carbon dioxide** – to pass easily between an animal's body and surrounding water. The gas exchange is the equivalent of breathing underwater. No mammals have developed gills, but gills are common among freshwater insects, especially in their underwater immature stages (larvae).

Of all the animals to have colonised freshwaters, fish and insects are probably the most successful. Some 10,000 species of fish of all kinds live in freshwater. Insect types that have made freshwaters their own include dragonflies, mayflies, mosquitoes and midges, caddis flies, bugs and beetles. On the left, a brown trout leaps to catch a damselfly.

RIFT VALLEY LAKES

The lakes in the Great Rift Valley region of Africa are surrounded by biomes ranging from desert to rainforest. Hippopotamuses, crocodiles, flamingos and an array of colourful fish are some of the lakes' varied residents.

Fact File

▲ The Rift Valley lakes of East Africa formed 3–7 million years ago when upheavals in Earth's crust created a chain of deep valleys and mountains.

▲ In some lakes, such as Lakes Tanganyika and Malawi, the water has separate layers that do not mix. Beneath the surface layer there is no oxygen and the water is saturated with toxic hydrogen sulfide, so animals stay in the surface layer and avoid the depths.

▲ At 1,435 metres (4,700 feet, or nearly 1 mile) deep, Lake Tanganyika is the second deepest lake in the world, after Lake Baikal in Russia.

Victorian Fish

Lake Victoria, the largest lake in Africa, lies between the two arms of East Africa's Great Rift Valley. It is much shallower than lakes Tanganyika and Malawi, which lie in the Rift Valley itself. Although it was formed only 200,000 years ago, Lake Victoria, like lakes Tanganyika and Malawi, supports hundreds of species of fish. Most are members of the cichlid fish family and are found nowhere else. It is a mystery how so many species evolved in so short a time. Fishing has always been important to the local human population, and to improve the catch of fish, the lake's residents introduced a large predatory fish in the 1950s. Called the Nile perch, this fish has since eaten its way through the native cichlids. The lake has also suffered from pollution by sewage and fertilisers from farms. This, together with modern fishing techniques and hungry Nile perches, has led to the tragic extinction of perhaps two-thirds of Lake Victoria's 500 or so native fish species.

Fishing communities line the shores of Lake Victoria. The people fish either from large trawlers or from canoes (below). They often equip the canoes with sails.

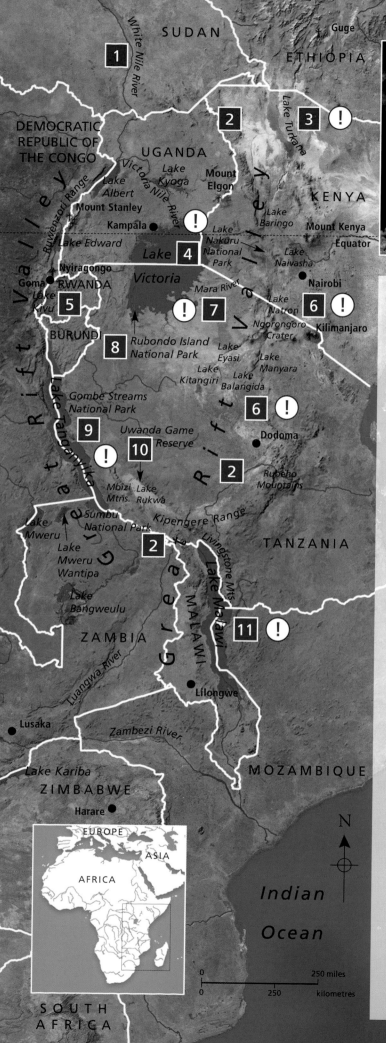

Above: just one of the hundreds of amazing cichlid fish species living in Lake Malawi, this one broods its young in its mouth.

1. Nile River
The source of the Nile River is a stream flowing into Lake Victoria. When the river leaves the lake, it flows northward for 6,400 kilometres (4,000 miles) to the Mediterranean Sea.

2. Great Rift Valleys
Forces deep inside Earth created this split down East Africa. Water collected in the deepest valleys and formed the Rift Valley lakes.

3. Lake Turkana
Until two million years ago, this lake was freshwater and connected to the Nile. Now its soda waters have a rich growth of algae and cyanobacteria that feed shrimps that, in turn, feed flamingos. A dam being built in Ethiopia on the Omo River will affect water supply to the lake.

4. Lake Victoria
Africa's largest lake is also the second biggest freshwater body in the world by area after Lake Superior, although its greatest depth is only 80 metres (250 feet). Invasive water hyacinths form thick mats on the lake, stifling aquatic life by blocking sunlight to the water below.

5. Lake Kivu
This lake was formed when lava dammed a river valley around 20,000 years ago. In January 2002, lava from the Nyiragongo volcano flowed into the lake, after first devastating the nearby city of Goma.

6. Eastern Rift Valley Lakes
Some of these lakes are freshwater, some are salty, and others are soda lakes. They are home to flamingos, which move between the lakes. Lakes Manyara and Nakuru are both national parks. Pollution, deforestation, and invasive species threaten wildlife there.

7. Mara River
Every year millions of migrating wildebeest cross this river. Crocodiles hide in the water at crossings, waiting for a meal. In recent years, the river has been lower than usual, probably because of global warming.

8. Rubondo Island National Park
This island in Lake Victoria is best known for its rich bird life.

9. Lake Tanganyika
This deep lake has a relatively small human population living on its shores. Its deepest point lies far below sea level and is also the lowest point on the African continent. It is home to hundreds of cichlid fish species. Overfishing threatens fish stocks.

10. Uwanda Game Reserve
This reserve includes most of Lake Rukwa, a salt lake noted for its bird life and a large population of crocodiles.

11. Lake Malawi
Lake Malawi contains more fish species than all of Europe's and North America's rivers and lakes put together. Malawi's 600 or more cichlid fish include some that eat only fish scales and others that nibble other fish's fins. Pollution and overfishing are beginning to put pressure on the lake's unique wildlife.

Murky Waters

Rivers vary in how much sediment (mud, sand, gravel or boulders) they carry, and the animals that live in them reflect this. So when people change the sediment entering a river, they change its wildlife. When settlers first plowed the land around the Mississippi for crops, soil was washed into streams, smothering native species, such as freshwater mussels and clogging up gravel beds where fish lay their eggs. When it reached the coast, the Mississippi's sediment once dispersed into the sea and over thousands of years it built the Mississippi Delta (right). Today, the river is artificially channeled through its delta. The sediment is no longer dispersed, so the delta is now shrinking.

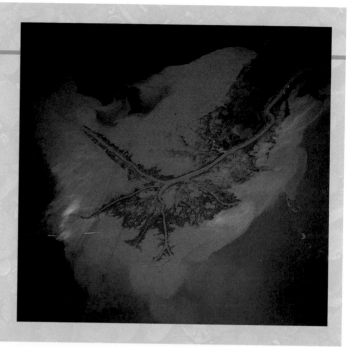

The Huang He (Yellow River) is a turbulent and unpredictable river that freezes over in its middle section each winter. Nevertheless, people have used it for travel for thousands of years, and it flows near some of China's oldest cities.

it is an oily fish and must be smoked to preserve it. So people have to cut down many trees for firewood, resulting in more damage to the environment.

Fish and other animals are sometimes introduced to new habitats accidentally. The sea lamprey – a sucker-mouthed fish that rasps the flesh of trout and other fish – probably got into the Great Lakes via canals, which provided a bypass around Niagara Falls. Once there, the lamprey virtually wiped out the lakes' trout; today, it is finally being brought under control. The zebra mussel is another notorious invader. It and many other recent arrivals probably got to the Great Lakes via the ballast water that ships take in to weigh themselves down. The salty water of the Caspian Sea has been invaded by a jellyfish-like animal called a comb jelly, which somehow got there from North American coastal waters.

Above: fishers on the Congo River display a Nile perch, which lives in several major African rivers. When introduced to lakes, it usually wreaks ecological havoc.

Rivers, Lakes and Recreation

Rivers and lakes are increasingly used for recreation. Houseboating vacations and cruises are popular on many rivers and lakes in the United States, including Lake Shasta, California, Lake Travis, Texas, and the Mississippi River. From the 1960s onwards in the United Kingdom, disused canals gained a new lease of life when people began using them for narrowboat vacations. Others use rivers and lakes for kayaking and canoeing. The more adventurous can try their hand at whitewater rafting or water skiing. Many rivers and lakes are used by bathers and swimmers. In addition, angling is a popular hobby in many countries of the world, including the United States.

Although the recreational use of rivers and lakes can cause some damage and pollution, its benefits to wildlife outweigh the drawbacks. These areas become protected and managed, which allows their plants and animals to thrive.

HUANG HE AND CHANG

China has a very long history, and its two greatest rivers, the Huang He (Yellow River) and the Chang (Yangtze), have been bound up with the fortunes of its peoples for thousands of years.

The Three Gorges Dam

The massive Three Gorges Dam built on the Chang River has been an extremely controversial project. The developers had several aims: to use turbines in the dam to generate electricity, to help ships pass up the river, to control floods and to allow diversion of river water to other areas. The spectacular Three Gorges have not been submerged, because their walls are up to 1,200 metres (4,000 feet) high and the river level has risen much less than this. The flooded area was the home of people for thousands of years. In addition, there is cultural loss due to ancient towns and cities being flooded. The main body of the dam was finished in 2006 and is now being used to generate electricity. The project will be completed in 2011. The dam is thought to have contributed to the extinction of the baiji, or Yangtze river dolphin.

1. Tibetan Plateau
The highest plateau in the world is the source of many of Asia's greatest rivers, including the rivers of China. Glaciers that feed the rivers are retreating because of global warming.

2. Tanggula Shan
The Chang (Yangtze) River begins as meltwater from snow and glaciers on the high Tanggula Shan mountains. The water forms streams that flow across the Tibetan Plateau. Again, glaciers are retreating.

3. Brahmaputra River
This great river starts in Tibet. There are fears in India that the Chinese government is planning to divert some of its waters to the Chang.

4. Mekong River
A river very rich in animal life, especially its fish species. Chinese dams greatly impact countries further downstream.

5. Yunnan-Guizhou Plateau
Rivers of the Chang system cut deep gorges through this

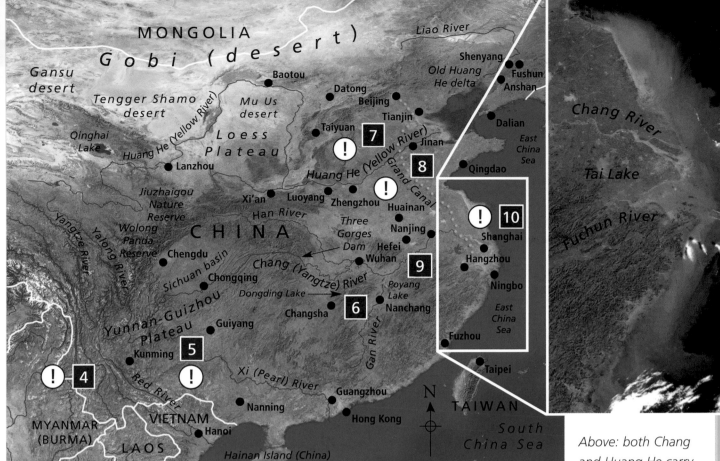

MONGOLIA
G o b i (d e s e r t)
Liao River

Gansu
desert
Shenyang
Old Huang
He delta
Fushun
Anshan
Baotou
Datong
Beijing
Tengger Shamo
desert
Mu Us
desert
Dalian
East
China
Sea
Qinghai
Lake
Taiyuan
Tianjin
7
Loess
Plateau
Huang He (Yellow River)
Jinan
Lanzhou
8
Qingdao
Jiuzhaigou
Nature
Reserve
Xi'an
Luoyang
Zhengzhou
Huang He (Yellow River)
Grand Canal
Huainan
Han River
10
Wolong
Panda
Reserve
C H I N A
Three
Gorges
Dam
Nanjing
Shanghai
Chengdu
Hefei
Wuhan
Hangzhou
Yangtze River
Yalong River
Sichuan basin
Chang (Yangtze) River
Chongqing
Ningbo
Dongding Lake
Poyang
Lake
Nanchang
East
China
Sea
Yunnan-Guizhou
Plateau
Changsha
6
Guiyang
Gan River
Fuzhou
Kunming
5
4
Red River
Xi (Pearl) River
Taipei
N
Nanning
Guangzhou
TAIWAN
MYANMAR
(BURMA)
LAOS
VIETNAM
Hanoi
Hong Kong
South
China Sea
Hainan Island (China)

Chang River
Tai Lake
Fuchun River

Above: both Chang and Huang He carry a heavy load of sediment. Here, the Chang dumps yellow sediment at its mouth in the East China Sea.

Below: the Huang He is a muddy torrent in the wet season, but in some years it dries up before reaching the sea.

limestone region and also flow underground through caverns. Many rare animals are found here. Deforestation and pollution threaten this region.

6. Lakes Region
The lakes of this populous, fertile region help to absorb the Chang's floodwater. Wildlife swims into the lakes during floods and back to the river in the dry season.

7. Huang He (Yellow River)
The Huang He sometimes causes enormous floods. The Chinese have been trying flood controls for thousands of years. Pollution is a serious problem in the Yellow River.

8. Grand Canal
More than 2,000 years old, the Grand Canal joins the Chang with the Huang He. The water is severely polluted in places.

9. Lower Chang River
Endangered animals live here, including the finless porpoise and the Chinese alligator.

10. Shanghai
China's largest city lies near the mouth of the Chang. If water is diverted northward from the Chang, seawater may seep into the Shanghai area to replace the freshwater, affecting water supplies.

 Fact File

▲ At 6,300 kilometres (3,915 miles) long, the Chang is Asia's longest river.

▲ China has some highly polluted rivers. The pollution comes from factories, agricultural fertilisers washing into rivers and sewage.

▲ The sediments laid down by the Huang He often cause its river channel to be higher than the surrounding countryside – one reason why its floods can be so disastrous.

There are many lakes and ponds across the world that are so polluted by fertilizers and wastes that fish and amphibians can no longer survive in them.

no access to safe drinking water and are in urgent need of better supplies. Furthermore, more of the world's people are living in cities. Due to the high-energy urban lifestyle, the average city dweller uses much more water in the home than a person living in the country.

Signs of Hope

There is a brighter side, however. To begin with, we're beginning to understand how freshwater ecosystems work, and so are more aware of the damage our actions might do. Today, for example, any major new dam proposal usually results in an international outcry at least. In the United States, the

Climate Change

Global warming is the gradual warming of the Earth's climate caused by the emission of carbon dioxide, methane, and other "greenhouse gases" from industry, transportation, energy generation, and agriculture. Most scientists now agree that global warming is causing widespread climate change. It is having serious effects on all biomes, including rivers and lakes. In many places, global warming is melting the glaciers, rivers of ice, that are the sources of many of the world's major rivers. This increases the rivers' flow and causes flooding. Global warming is also altering the pattern of the world's rainfall, resulting in unpredictable changes to river and lake levels and lake saltiness. In the short term, it appears to be making dry places drier and wet places wetter. Worldwide, governments are working together to combat their nations' emissions of greenhouse gases. But at present they cannot agree on many measures and targets. Scientists and other people fear that not enough is being done.

passing of the Clean Water Act in 1972 was a first step toward tackling the problem of pollution in the nation's rivers and lakes. Local action has resulted in the cleaning up of many rivers—the Charles River in Massachusetts is a well-known example. Many older dams have also been dismantled in states such as Maine and California, allowing rivers to run freely again and enabling migratory fish such as salmon to swim up them to breed. Animals such as the American alligator have also benefited from new laws protecting them from exploitation.

In England, a homely but welcome development has been the growing popularity of garden ponds—these have done much to preserve populations of frogs and newts threatened by the destruction of pond habitats in the countryside.

There may be bright aspects to the long-term future, too. For example, much electricity currently comes from hydropower, which is cheap and clean but can disrupt freshwater ecosystems drastically. If we're lucky, even cheaper, cleaner power may one day become available from a process called nuclear fusion, which is still in its preliminary experimental stages but would produce far less pollution than today's nuclear power stations.

Lake Superior is at the heart of one of the world's largest freshwater ecosystems. As more people come to enjoy its wild beauty and its unrivaled leisure facilities, shoreline developments are damaging fish spawning grounds, amphibian habitats, and bird nesting sites.

Saving the Planet

In the United States, the federal Clean Water Act allows citizens to take action to clean up their own watersheds. The powers it gives center around the concept of a "total maximum daily load" of pollution. Called TMDL for short, this is the amount of pollution that any river or lake can take while still remaining healthy, wherever the pollution happens to come from. Using Clean Water Act legislation, citizens can monitor TMDL reports for their local watershed and force states and local governments to come up with an action plan to reduce pollution. This safeguards the health not only of fish and other freshwater animals but also that of the people who use the water for bathing and drinking.